CHEETAH

Curious Kids Press

Cheetahs

Cheetahs are a large wild cat. It was highly regarded by man and dates back as far as 3,000 BC with the Sumerians. The cheetah has been depicted in paintings and were even tamed and kept as pets for royalty. This animal was also thought to have the ability to carry away someone's soul after death. For this reason, many paintings and statues were placed in the tombs of Pharaohs. Read on to discover more cool cheetah facts.

Where in the World?

Did you know the cheetah will live in many different habitats? This wild cat likes to spend time in mountainous terrains, open or grassy plains and even in dense forests. It can be found in some areas of Africa and Asia. The cheetah's numbers have declined and it is now considered endangered.

The Body of a Cheetah

Did you know the cheetah is often mistaken for a leopard? Both of these wild cats have spots, but the cheetah is smaller than a leopard. Male cheetahs are slightly larger than females. He can weigh up to 140 pounds. The cheetah also has long slender legs and is tan in color.

The Coat of a Cheetah

Did you know the cheetah has black spots? The coat of the cheetah is covered with black spots, but it does not have any on its belly. On each side of the cheetah's nose (from the corner of its eyes to its mouth) there are 2 black lines. These are called "tear marks." It also has black rings around its tail.

What a Cheetah Eats

Did you know cheetahs eat meat? This carnivore will hunt larger prey like wildebeest calves, impalas, gazelles, antelope and rabbits. The cheetah will eat about 6 to 8 pounds of meat each day. It will eat its kill very quickly, to avoid losing it to other predators, such as a lion.

The Cheetah's Special Ability

Did you know the cheetah is super fast? In fact, it is the world's fastest land mammal. This large cat can reach speeds of up to 70 miles-per-hour. However, it cannot keep this speed up and will tire very quickly. It can also go from 0 to 40 miles-per-hour in 3 strides.

The Cheetah as a Predator

Did you know the cheetah doesn't always catch its prey? This cat uses it super-speed to catch its meal. The cheetah gets as close as possible, then bursts into a full run. It will then trip the animal with its front paw. Once the animal falls, the cheetah bites its throat and will hold onto it until it has died.

The Cheetah as Prey

Did you know it is illegal to kill a cheetah? Humans have hunted the cheetah for its coat. It is now protected by law. For this reason the cheetah's numbers have declined over the years. Another predator of the cheetah are lions. Adult lions will sometimes hunt old, sick, injured or even baby cheetahs.

The Cheetah Territory

Did you know the female cheetah prefers to live alone? After the mother cheetah has raised her young, she will go off to be on her own again. Her territory can range from 30 square miles up to over 1,800 square miles. She doesn't defend her territory, but some male cheetahs will defend their own.

Cheetah Talk

Did you know cheetahs can make sounds? Unlike some large cats, the cheetah cannot roar. But it can make other sounds. A cheetah will hiss, growl and whine when it is upset. Mother cheetahs will purr with her cubs. Plus, all cheetahs make a bird-like chirping call. This may be used as a greeting.

The Cheetah Mom

Did you know the female cheetah can become pregnant any time of the year? The female cheetah is ready to have young at around 2 years-old. Once she becomes pregnant, she will carry her cubs for about 3 months before giving birth to them. The cubs are born in a safe den away from predators.

The Cheetah Baby

Did you know baby cheetahs look like honey badgers? Cheetah cubs are very fuzzy and have long silver-grey hair that stands up along their backs. This makes them look like a fierce honey badger so predators will not want them. The cubs will start to eat meat at 4 to 6 weeks of age.

Cheetahs at Rest

Did you know cheetahs are diurnal? This means they hunt their prey in the early morning and late afternoon. When a cheetah is not hunting it will rest under trees or wherever it decides to. Cheetahs also need to rest after a hunt. In fact, they are so spent they often lose their kill to lions or a pack of hungry hyenas.

Cheetahs at Play

Did you know cheetah cubs learn to hunt through playing? Like other cats, cheetah cubs will learn to run, stalk and pounce through play. The cubs play with each other and also with their mother. Baby cheetahs practice their skills until they are old enough to hunt on their own.

Life of a Cheetah

Did you know male cheetahs will form small groups? Some male cheetahs don't mind living with each other. These small groups are usually all brothers from the same litter. Cheetahs in the wild can live to be around 8 to 12 years-old, but in zoos and animal preserves, they can live up to 20 years-old.

Quiz

Question 1: Where are the "tear marks" located on the cheetah?

Answer 1: On its face

Question 2: The cheetah is the world's fastest land animal. How fast can it run?

Answer 2: It can reach speeds of 70 miles-per-hour

Question 3: What time of the year can the female cheetah become pregnant?

Answer 3: Anytime of the year

Question 4: What other animal does the baby cheetah look like?

Answer 4: It looks like a honey badger

Question 5: How long can a cheetah live in captivity?

Answer 5: Up to 20 years-old

Thank you for checking out another addition from Curious Kids Press! Make sure to check out Amazon.com for many other great titles.

Made in the USA
Las Vegas, NV
29 March 2022